TOMAC'S PUMPKIN (AND SQUASH) COOKBOOK

ISSUED AND COPYRIGHTED 2022
BY SARAH AND PENNIE TOMAC
PHOTOS BY SARAH TOMAC

copyright April 1, 2022
by Sarah J Tomac
Tomac Pumpkins
Chesaning, Michigan
in conjunction with 1831 Press
ALL RIGHTS RESERVED

No part of this book may be reproduced or transmitted in any form or means without written consent from the author and publisher

All content is original work
Photographed and Edited By: Sarah Tomac

Print IBSN: 978-1-952265-04-4
E-book IBSN: 978-1-952265-05-1

CONTENTS

Page	Section
5	Drinks and Snacks
13	Soups
	Side Dishes
41	Savory
49	Sweet
53	Main Dishes
67	Cakes Cookies and Bars
77	Pies, Cheesecakes and Desserts
89	Index of Recipes
92	Index by Types of Pumpkin and Squash Used in Recipes
99	How To....Roast, Store, Puree a pumpkin and other useful tips

These Pages have room for your personal notes - write which type you liked to use best or which one your family always requests or add your own recipe!

HONEY ORANGE GINGER PUMPKIN BUTTER

6 cups pumpkin purée
1 cup orange juice
1 cup apple cider
3/4 cup honey
1/2 to 1 teaspoon cinnamon
1/2 to 1 teaspoon ginger

Combine ingredients.
Pour into a crock pot; low setting is best, leaving the lid slightly ajar.
Simmer, stirring occasionally until the desired thickness.
If needed, add more cider if the consistency thickens too much.

Yield: About 9 cups

PUMPKIN CHEESE BALL

8-ounce package cream cheese, softened
1/2 cup pumpkin purée
8 ounce can crushed pineapple, well drained
2 cups (8 ounces) shredded sharp cheddar cheese
1 package (2 1/2 ounces dried beef, finely chopped)
1 tablespoon finely chopped onion
Celery leaves
Assorted crackers and/or raw vegetables

In a mixing bowl, beat cream cheese, pumpkin and pineapple.
Stir in cheddar cheese, beef and onion.
Shape into a ball; place on a serving platter.
Scrape sides with a knife to resemble a pumpkin and add celery leaves for a stem.
Serve with crackers and/or vegetables.

Yield: 3 cups

PUMPKIN HARVEST DIP

8 ounces cream cheese, softened
2 cups confectioners' sugar
2 cups pumpkin purée
3 teaspoons pumpkin pie spice
1 teaspoon vanilla
1/2 teaspoon ground ginger
Apple and pear slices and/or ginger snap cookies, animal crackers, pretzels for dipping

In a large mixing bowl, beat the cream cheese and confectioners' sugar.
Gradually add the pumpkin, pie spice, vanilla and ginger; beat until smooth.
Serve with fruit or other crackers or cookies.
Refrigerate leftovers.

Yield: 3 1/2 cups

PUMPKIN HUMMUS

2 cans (15 ounces each) garbanzo beans or chickpeas, rinsed and drained
2 cups pumpkin purée
1/2 cup olive oil
1/3 cup tahini
5 tablespoons lemon juice
2 teaspoons hot pepper sauce
2 garlic cloves, minced
1 teaspoon salt
Baked pita chips
Assorted fresh vegetables, optional

Place the first eight ingredients in a food processor;
Cover and process until blended.
Serve with pita chips and fresh vegetables as desired.

Yield: 4 cups

PUMPKIN PIE SMOOTHIE

1 carton (5.3 ounces) fat-free plain Greek yogurt
1/2 cup 2% milk
2 tablespoons maple syrup
1/4 teaspoon ground cinnamon or pumpkin pie spice
2 teaspoons almond butter or peanut butter
2/3 cup pumpkin purée
1 cup ice cubes
1 tablespoon granola

Place first seven ingredients in a blender;
Cover and process until blended.
Pour into glasses; top with granola.

Yield: 2 servings

How To Prepare Seeds:
Wash Pumpkin and split open, (cut or smash)
Remove Seeds by hand into bowl
Rinse the seeds in cold water and remove the strings and pulp.
Roast directly or spread to dry the cleaned seeds on a nonstick surface.
(They will stick to paper toweling and cannot be removed without bits of paper sticking to them).

There are naked seeded or hulless varieties of pumpkins that are very good for making pumpkin seeds as they do not have the hard, thick seed coats that most of the pumpkins and squash have.

They are also called pepitas.

ROASTED PUMPKIN SEEDS

2 CUPS CLEANED PUMPKIN SEEDS
1/2 TABLESPOON MELTED BUTTER OR OLIVE OIL
SALT

Preheat oven to 250*F.
Lightly grease baking sheet.
Mix seeds and melted butter or oil in a small bowl until seeds are coated.
Spread pumpkin seeds onto non-stick baking sheet.
Sprinkle desired amount of salt over seeds
Bake, stirring often, until seeds are dry and lightly browned, about 1 hour.
Remove from oven. Cool.
Serve. Stored cover in glass or plastic food container.

SPICY PUMPKIN SEEDS

2 CUPS FRESH PUMPKIN SEEDS
1/2 TABLESPOON MELTED BUTTER OR OLIVE OIL
1 TEASPOON WORCESTER SAUCE
1 TEASPOON SUGAR
1/2 TEASPOON SALT
1/4 TEASPOON GARLIC POWDER
1/8 TEASPOON GROUND RED PEPPER

Preheat oven to 250*F.
Lightly grease baking sheet.
Mix all ingredients in a small bowl until seeds are coated.
Spread pumpkin seeds onto non-stick baking sheet.
Bake, stirring often, until seeds are dry and lightly browned, about 1 hour.
Remove from oven. Cool.
Serve. Stored cover in glass or plastic food container.

Yield: 4 servings.

FROSTED PUMPKIN DOUGHNUTS

2 eggs
1 cup sugar
2 tablespoons butter or margarine, softened
1 cup pumpkin purée
1 tablespoon lemon juice
4 1/2 cups flour
2 teaspoons baking powder
1 teaspoon baking soda
1/2 teaspoon salt
1/2 teaspoon cinnamon
1/2 teaspoon nutmeg
1 cup evaporated milk
Oil for deep-fat frying

Frosting:
3 cups confectioners' sugar
2 to 3 tablespoons orange juice
1 tablespoon evaporated milk
1 teaspoon grated orange peel

In a mixing bowl, beat eggs, sugar and butter.
Add pumpkin and lemon juice; mix well.
Combine the dry ingredients; add to pumpkin mixture alternately with milk.
Cover and refrigerate for 2 hours.
Turn onto a lightly floured surface; knead 5-6 times.
Roll out to a 3/8-inch thickness.
Cut with a 2 1/2-inch doughnut cutter.
In an electric skillet or deep fat fryer, heat oil to 375*F.
Fry doughnuts, about 3 minutes, until golden; turn once with a slotted spoon.
Drain on paper towels.

Combine frosting ingredients; spread over cooled doughnuts.

Yield: about 3 dozen.

OATMEAL PUMPKIN BREAD

1 cup uncooked quick-cooking oats
1 cup milk heated
3/4 cup pumpkin purée
2 eggs, beaten
1/4 cup margarine, melted and cooled
1 teaspoon vanilla extract
2 cups flour
1 cup sugar
1 tablespoon baking powder
1/4 teaspoon salt
1 teaspoon cinnamon
1/4 teaspoon ground nutmeg
1/8 teaspoon ground cloves

1 cup raisins
2/3 cup chopped pecans

Preheat oven to 350 degrees F.
Grease a 9 x 5- inch loaf baking pan.
Mix oats and milk in a large bowl, let stand for 5 minutes.
Stir in pumpkin, eggs, margarine, and vanilla extract.
Mix flour, sugar, baking powder, salt, cinnamon, nutmeg, and cloves in another bowl;
Gradually stir the mixture into oat mixture.
Stir in raisins and pecans.
Spread batter into prepared baking pan.
Bake 55-60 minutes or until a wooden pick inserted in center comes out clean.
Cool in pan for 5 minutes.
Remove from pan; cool on wire rack.
Refrigerate leftovers.

Yield: 1 loaf

PUMPKIN BREAD

3 cups sugar
1 cup cooking oil
4 eggs
3 1/3 cups flour
2 teaspoons baking soda
1 1/2 teaspoons salt
1 teaspoon cinnamon
1 teaspoon nutmeg
2/3 cup water
2 cups pumpkin purée

Preheat oven to 350*F.
Grease bottoms and sides of three 8 x 4 x 2 inch loaf pans; set aside.
In an extra-large mixing bowl beat sugar and oil with an electric mixer on medium speed.
Add eggs and pumpkin and beat well; set aside.
Combine the flour, soda, salt, cinnamon and nutmeg.
Add dry mixture and water alternately to sugar mixture, beating on low speed after each addition just until combined.
Spoon batter into prepared pans.
Bake in a 350 degrees F oven 55 to 60 minutes or until wooden toothpick inserted in center comes out clean.
Cool for 10 minutes, remove pans.
Cool, wrap and store overnight before storing or freeze for later use.

YIELD: makes 3 loaves.

VARIATIONS: stir in chocolate chips or dried fruit like raisins, cranberries, dates and/or nuts.

LOAF PAN alternative size: 7 x 3 x 2-inch FOUR (4) PANS WILL BE NEEDED

PUMPKIN CHIP MUFFINS

1 3/4 cups flour
1 teaspoon baking powder
1 teaspoon baking soda
1/2 teaspoon salt
1/2 teaspoon cinnamon
1/4 teaspoon nutmeg
2 eggs, lightly beaten
1/2 cup honey
1/2 cup vegetable oil
1 cup pumpkin purée
1/3 cup water
1 cup miniature chocolate chips

Preheat oven to 350*F
Sift together the flour, baking powder, soda, salt and spices.
Combine the eggs, pumpkin, oil, honey, and water.
Mix well.
Stir into the dry ingredients just until combined; fold in chocolate chips.
Fill greased muffin pans 2/3 full.
Bake for 20 to 25 minutes.

Yield: Makes 12 to 15 large muffins.

PUMPKIN CORN BREAD

1/3 cup corn oil
1 cup flour
1 cup cornmeal
1 1/4 teaspoon baking soda
1/2 teaspoon salt
1 cup pumpkin purée
1/2 cup buttermilk
2 eggs
2 tablespoons brown sugar

Brush the inside of a 9–10-inch cast iron skillet with 1 tablespoon of the oil.
Place in the oven; set the oven temperature to 425*F.
In a large bowl, sift together the flour, cornmeal, baking soda, and salt.
In a separate bowl, combine the pumpkin, buttermilk, remaining oil, eggs, and brown sugar.
Then stir the dry ingredients into the wet until just combined.
Remove the skillet from the oven, pour in the batter,
Return to the oven and bake 30-40 minutes, until the center is firm.
Serve warm in wedges.

Yield: 8-10 servings

PUMPKIN MUFFINS

2 cups sifted flour
2 teaspoons baking powder
1/2 teaspoon salt
1/2 teaspoon ginger
1/2 teaspoon ground nutmeg
1/8 teaspoon ground cloves
1/3 cup raisins or dried cranberries (optional)
1/3 cup butter, softened
3/4 cup brown sugar
1/4 cup molasses (dark preferred)
2 beaten eggs
1 cup pumpkin purée
1/2 cup milk

Preheat over to 375*F
Sift together the flour, baking powder, salt and spices.
Add the raisins and coat well.
Cream the sugar, butter and molasses,
Add the milk, eggs, and pumpkin and blend well.
Stir in the dry ingredients, blending only till moistened.
Fill greased muffin pans 2/3 full.
Bake for 16 to 18 minutes.

Yield: makes 12 to 15 large muffins

PUMPKIN PANCAKES

2 CUPS FLOUR
1 1/2 TEASPOONS BAKING POWDER
1/2 TEASPOON BAKING SODA
1 TEASPOON PUMPKIN PIE SPICE
1/2 TEASPOON SALT
4 TABLESPOONS BROWN SUGAR
3 LARGE EGGS
1 2/3 CUPS BUTTERMILK
3/4 CUP PUMPKIN PURÉE
4 TABLESPOONS BUTTER, MELTED
CANOLA OIL
PURE MAPLE SYRUP

Preheat oven to 250*F.
In a large bowl, combine the flour, baking powder, baking soda, pie spices and salt.
In a separate bowl mix the sugar and eggs until well blended.
Stir in the buttermilk, pumpkin and butter.
Add the dry ingredients into the wet and mix until smooth.
Heat a griddle or cast-iron pan over moderately high heat.
Brush lightly with oil, drop batter by 1/4 cupfuls onto the griddle.
Cook pancakes until bubbles form on top and bottoms are golden brown.
Turn pancakes over.
Cook until bottoms are golden brown.
Transfer to a sheet pan and place in the oven to keep warm.
Repeat with remaining batter.
Serve pancakes hot, with maple syrup.

YIELD: MAKES 12 PANCAKES, SERVES 4

RIBBON PUMPKIN BREAD

FILLING:
8 ounces cream cheese, softened
1/4 cup sugar
1 tablespoon flour
1 egg

BATTER:
1 cup pumpkin purée
1/2 cup unsweetened applesauce
2 eggs
1 tablespoon canola oil
1 2/3 cup flour
1 1/4 cup sugar
1 teaspoon baking soda
1/2 teaspoon salt
1/2 teaspoon cinnamon
1/2 teaspoon cloves
1/3 cup chopped walnuts (optional)

For filling, combine the cream cheese, sugar, flour and eggs in a bowl; set aside.

Preheat oven 350*F
In a mixing bowl, beat the pumpkin, applesauce, eggs and oil.
Combine the flour, sugar, baking soda, salt, cinnamon and cloves;
Add to pumpkin mixture.
Stir in walnuts.
Divide half of the batter between two 8 x 4 x 2-inch greased loaf pans.
Spread each with filling; top with remaining batter.
Bake for 40-45 minutes or until a toothpick inserted near the center comes out clean.
Cool for 10 minutes before removing from pans to wire rack to cool completely.

Refrigerate leftovers.

YIELD: 2 loaves

YEAST BREADS

BUTTERCUP SQUASH BREAD

1 package active dry yeast
1/2 cup warm water
2 tablespoons molasses
1 teaspoon salt
1 teaspoon caraway seeds
1 cup mashed cooked buttercup squash
3 cups all-purpose flour, divided

In a large bowl, mix yeast with warm water until dissolved.
Add molasses, salt, caraway seeds, squash and 2 cups flour; mix well.
Add enough remaining flour to form soft dough.
Place dough on a floured surface; knead until smooth and elastic, about 8 minutes.
Place dough in a large greased bowl, turning once to grease top.
Cover with a clean kitchen towel and let rise until doubled in size, about an hour.
Punch dough down and place on a floured surface.
Shape into a loaf.
Placed in a greased 9 x 5-inch loaf pan.
Cover with a clean kitchen towel and let rise until double in size, about 45 minutes.

Preheat oven to 400*F.
Bake bread 25-30 minutes or until golden brown.
Remove from oven and immediately remove from pan.
Cool on wire rack. Refrigerate leftovers.

Yield: 16 slices.

Buttercup squash is a drier squash, if you use a different kind of squash, you may need additional flour.

PUMPKIN KNOT ROLLS

2 packages active dry yeast
1 cup warm milk
1/3 cup butter or margarine, softened
1/2 cup sugar
1 cup pumpkin purée
3 eggs
1 1/2 teaspoons salt
5 1/2 to 6 cups flour
1 tablespoon cold water
Sesame or poppy seeds, optional

In a mixing bowl, dissolve yeast in warm milk.
Add the butter, sugar, pumpkin, 2 eggs, salt and 3 cups flour.
Beat until smooth.
Stir in enough remaining flour to form soft dough.
Turn onto a lightly floured surface; knead until smooth and elastic, about 6-8 minutes.
Place in a greased bowl, turning once to grease top.
Cover and let rise in a warm place until doubled, about 1 hour.
Punch dough down. Turn onto a lightly floured surface and divide in half.
Shape each portion into 12 balls.
Roll each ball into a 10-inch rope; tie into a knot and tuck ends under.
Place 2 inches apart on greased baking sheets.
Cover and let rise until doubled, about 30 minutes.
In a small bowl, beat water and remaining egg.
Brush over rolls. Sprinkle with sesame or poppy seeds if desired.
Bake at 350*F for 15-20 minutes or until golden brown.
Remove from pans to wire racks.

Yield: 2 dozen.

PUMPKIN-RAISIN YEAST BREAD

3 ½-CUPS ALL-PURPOSE FLOUR
2 PACKAGES ACTIVE DRY YEAST
¼ TSP GINGER
¼ TSP NUTMEG
¼ TSP CLOVES
¾ CUP MILK
¼ CUP BROWN SUGAR
2 TBS BUTTER
1 ½ TSP SALT
½ CUP COOKED PUMPKIN
¾ CUP RAISINS

Combine 1 ½ cups flour, yeast and spices.
In sauce pan heat milk, butter, brown sugar, and salt until warm, stirring constantly.
Add to dry mixture.
Stir in pumpkin.
Beat well.
Stir in raisins and remaining flour.
Dough will be moderately stiff.
Turn onto floured surface and knead till smooth and elastic. (5 to 8 minutes).
Shape into ball and place in lightly greased bowl, turning once.
Cover, set in warm place and let rise until double in size. (about 1 hour).
Punch down.
Shape into loaf.
Place in greased 8 ½ x 4 ½ x 2 ½-inch loaf pan.
Cover. Let rise until double. (about 30 minutes).

Bake in 375*F oven 35 to 40 minutes.

PUMPKIN CINNAMON ROLLS

1 package yeast
1/2 cup warm water
2/3 cup oil
1/2 cup sugar
1 tablespoon salt
1 cup pumpkin puree
1 cup scalded milk
2 eggs beaten
6 cups flour (may need to add more)

Filliing:
Softened Butter
Brown Sugar
Cinnamon

Dissolve yeast in warm water
Mix ingredients and let rise for 1 hour
Roll out dough and spread with Bbutter, brown sugar and cinnamon.
Roll up lengthways and cut into 3/4 inch slices.
Place cut side up in greased pans and let rise in warm place about 1 hour.
Bake at 350* for 20 minutes.

APPLE PUMPKIN SOUP

2 cups finely chopped peeled tart apples
1/2 cup finely chopped onion
2 tablespoons butter
1 tablespoon flour
4 cups chicken broth
3 cups pumpkin purée
1/4 cup packed brown sugar
1/2 teaspoon ground cinnamon
1/2 teaspoon nutmeg
1/2 teaspoon ginger
1 cup unsweetened apple juice
1/2 cup half and half cream
1/4 teaspoon salt
1/4 teaspoon pepper

In a large saucepan on medium heat, sauté the apples and onion in butter for 3-5 minutes or until tender.
Stir in the flour until blended.
Gradually whisk in the chicken broth.
Stir in the pumpkin, brown sugar, cinnamon, nutmeg, and ginger.
Bring to a boil.
Reduce heat; cover and simmer for 25 minutes.
Cool slightly.
In a blender, cover and process soup in batches until smooth.
Pour into a bowl; cover and refrigerate for 8 hours or overnight.
Just before serving, transfer soup to a saucepan,
Heat over medium for 5-10 minutes
Stir in the apple juice, cream, salt and pepper; heat through.

Yield: 12 servings.

When processing soup in a blender it is important to cool slightly. If you do not let cool before processing, mixture will explode out of container and make a mess in the kitchen.

BEAN AND SQUASH SOUP

2 cups dry assorted beans, sorted, rinsed and drained
1 medium onion, chopped
1 medium butternut squash (or squash of your choice) peeled and diced
4 cups water
2 cups vegetable or chicken broth
2-3 cloves garlic, minced
1- 14 1/2 ounce can petite diced tomatoes
1 teaspoon ground cumin
1 teaspoon dried basil
1 teaspoon marjoram
1/8 teaspoon ground nutmeg
1 tablespoon lemon juice
Salt and pepper to taste
Sour cream

In a large soup pot over medium-high heat, place beans
Cover with cold water; bring to a boil.
Remove from heat; cover and let stand for 1-2 hours.
Drain and rinse beans.
In the same pot over medium heat, combine soaked beans, onion, squash, water, vegetable or chicken broth, garlic, tomatoes, cumin, basil, marjoram, and nutmeg.
Bring just to a boil;
Reduce heat and simmer 1 1/2 to 2 hours or until beans are tender.
Add lemon juice, salt and pepper.
Remove from heat and serve in soup bowls topped with sour cream, if desired.

Yield 4-6 servings.

Optional: add a few red pepper flakes to taste.

BLACK BEAN AND PUMPKIN CHILI

1 tablespoon olive oil
1 medium sweet yellow pepper, chopped
1 medium onion, chopped
3 garlic cloves, minced
3 cups chicken broth (reduced sodium preferred)
2 cups pumpkin or squash purée
1 can (14 1/2 ounces) diced tomatoes, undrained
2 teaspoons chili powder
1 1/2 teaspoons ground cumin
1 1/2 teaspoons dried oregano
1/2 teaspoon salt
1/2 teaspoon smoked paprika
2 cans (15 ounces each) black beans, rinsed and drained
1 1/2 cups shredded cooked chicken
1/4 cup chopped fresh cilantro or parsley.

In a large saucepan or stockpot, heat oil over medium heat.
Add pepper and onion; cook and stir 6-8 minutes or until tender.
Stir in garlic; cook 1 minute longer.
Stir in broth, pumpkin, tomatoes and seasonings.
Slightly mash half if the beans.
Add all beans to the pot; bring to a boil.
Reduce heat; simmer, covered for 45 minutes to allow the flavors to blend, stirring occasionally.
Stir in chicken and cilantro; heat throughout.

Yield: 8 servings

May also use peeled and diced squash/pumpkin.

BUTTERNUT BISQUE

2 MEDIUM CARROTS, SLICED
2 CELERY RIBS WITH LEAVES, CHOPPED
2 MEDIUM LEEKS (WHITE PORTION ONLY), SLICED
1 JALAPEÑO PEPPER, SEEDED AND MINCED
1/4 CUP BUTTER OR MARGARINE
2 POUNDS BUTTERNUT SQUASH, PEELED, SEEDED, AND CUBED (ABOUT 6 CUPS)
2 CANS (14 1/2 OUNCES) CHICKEN BROTH
1/2 TEASPOON GROUND GINGER
1/2 CUP HALF AND HALF CREAM
1/2 TEASPOON SALT
1/4 TEASPOON WHITE PEPPER
1/2 CUP TOASTED PUMPKIN SEEDS OR TOASTED PECANS

In a large saucepan, sauté carrots, celery, leeks and jalapeño in butter for 10 minutes, stirring occasionally.
Add the squash, broth and ginger; bring to a boil.
Reduce heat; cover and simmer until the squash is tender, about 25 minutes.
Cool until lukewarm in a blender or food processor, purée squash in small batches until smooth; return to the pan.
Add cream, salt and pepper; mix well.
Heat through but do not boil.
Garnish with pumpkin seeds or pecans.

YIELD: 8 SERVINGS.

CORN AND SQUASH SOUP

12 bacon strips, diced
1 medium onion, chopped
1 celery rib, chopped
2 tablespoons flour
1 can (14 1/2 ounces) chicken broth
6 cups mashed and cooked squash
2 cans cream style corn
2 cups half and half cream
1 tablespoon minced fresh parsley
1 1/2 teaspoons salt
1/2 teaspoon pepper
Sour Cream, optional.

In a large saucepan, cook bacon over medium heat until crisp.
Remove to paper towels; drain, reserving 2 tablespoons drippings.
In the drippings, sauté onion and celery until tender.
Stir in flour until blended.
Gradually stir in broth.
Bring to a boil; cook and stir for 2 minutes or until slightly thickened.
Reduce heat to medium.
Stir in the squash, corn, cream, parsley, salt, pepper and bacon.
Cook and stir until heated through.
Garnish with sour cream if desired.

Yield: 8 servings.

PUMPKIN SOUP WITH TORTELLINI

12 ounces beef tortellini
2 tablespoons olive oil
1 medium onion, chopped
1 clove garlic, minced
1/2 teaspoon ground coriander
1 teaspoon ground cumin
1 teaspoon cracked black peppercorns
1 pound pumpkin (squash), peeled and chopped
1 medium potato, peeled and cut into pieces
4 cups water 1 chicken stock cube
1/2 cup cream
1 tablespoon chopped, fresh chives
1 teaspoon chopped, fresh basil.

Cook tortellini in a large pan of boiling water, uncovered until just tender, drain and set aside.
Meanwhile, heat oil in pan; cook onion, garlic, coriander, and cumin; stirring until onion is tender.
Stir in peppercorns, pumpkin and potato, cook stirring 2 minutes.
Add water and stock cube, bring to a boil; simmer covered about 15 minutes or until vegetables are tender; cool slightly.
Blend or process mixture in batches until smooth.
Return soup to pan, stir in cream, herbs and tortellini; stir over heat until heated through.
Garnish with additional chives.

ROASTED SQUASH SOUP

1 butternut squash or squash of your choice
1 teaspoon + 2 tablespoons canola oil
1/2 cup diced onion
1/2 cup diced carrots
1/2 cup diced celery
1 tablespoon minced fresh ginger
5 cups vegetable broth
1 1/2 tablespoon ground cumin
2 teaspoons chili powder
1 teaspoon curry powder
1 teaspoon Old Bay Seasoning
1/2 teaspoon cayenne pepper
1/4 teaspoon cinnamon
2 teaspoons apple vinegar

Cut squash in half lengthwise.
Scoop seeds out.
Rub cut surface with 1 teaspoon oil.
Roast squash face down in a roasting pan until soft, cool and scoop flesh from skin.
In a soup or stock pot, heat remaining oil and sauté onion, carrots, and celery for 10-12 minutes.
Add 2 cups vegetable broth, scrape the bottom of the pan, then add squash. Stir, mixing squash and vegetables.
Blend 3 cups of the squash mixture at a time in a blender on high while adding more broth to thin out.
Return soup to a stock pot on medium low. Add rest of broth.
Bring soup to a simmer, add seasonings and let simmer for 10-15 minutes.
Taste and season with salt and pepper as needed. Serve hot.

Yield: 8 servings.

TURKEY BUTTERNUT SQUASH SOUP

A good way to use left-over turkey

1 tablespoon cooking oil
2 leeks, trimmed, chopped, and rinsed
1 red bell pepper, chopped
3 cloves fresh garlic, minced
4 cups chicken broth
1 1/2 pounds butternut squash, peeled, seeded and cut into 1-inch cubes.
2 teaspoons dried thyme leaves
1 1/2 teaspoons ground cumin
1-pound left-over turkey
2 cups frozen corn kernels
2 tablespoons fresh lime juice
1/2 teaspoon crushed red pepper
1/4 teaspoon salt, or to taste
1/4 teaspoon freshly ground black pepper, or to taste.

Heat cooking oil in a Dutch over medium-high heat.
Add leeks and red bell pepper; cook and stir until vegetables begin to soften, about 4 minutes.
Add garlic; cook and stir 1 minute.
Stir in broth, squash, thyme and cumin.
Cover and bring mixture to a boil.
Reduce heat to medium-low and cook until vegetables are tender, about 10 minutes.
Add turkey and corn.
Return to a simmer and heat through, about 5 minutes.
Stir in lime juice, crushed red pepper, salt and black pepper to taste.

Serve. Refrigerate leftovers.

PUMPKIN SOUP

1/2 pumpkin, medium size, cut into pieces
6 medium potatoes, cut into pieces
2 medium onions, diced
2 tablespoons of butter
1 teaspoon of good curry powder
Chicken Stock
Salt and pepper to taste
Sour Cream
Crumbled Crispy Bacon Pieces (optional)

Heat the camp oven over medium heat, melt the butter and saute the onion until softening
Add curry powder, stir through for 2-3 minutes
Add potato and Pumpkin pieces, cover with chicken stock and simmer until the vegetables are soft.
Puree with a stick blender (or mash by hand)
Add salt and pepper to taste.

Serve with a tablespoon of sour cream, sprinkled with bacon pieces

I use an enamaled Dutch Oven on my stove when not camping to make this recipe. Queensland Blue is the favorite pumpkin flavor to use, any will taste great.

Don't have Curry powder? a savory blend of your favorite seasoning works great too. add a little paprika and garlic to taste if curry powder is not available.

PUMPKIN (SQUASH) SIDE DISHES

SAVORY

CONCHIGLIE STUFFED WITH RICOTTA AND PUMPKIN

1/2-pound large Conchiglie (large pasta shells)
1 cup pumpkin purée
1 cup ricotta
1 cup grated Parmesan cheese
1 egg yolks
Large pinch nutmeg
Salt and white pepper
1 cup heavy cream

Cook the conchiglie in plenty of salted boiling water until al dente.
Drain in a colander and cool under cold running water.
In a medium bowl, combine the pumpkin purée, ricotta, 1/2 cup Parmesan, egg yolks, and nutmeg.
Season with salt and pepper to taste.
Fill the shells with this mixture.
Preheat oven to 375*F.
Lightly butter an 8 x 12-inch baking dish.
Arrange the stuffed shells in the dish.
In a small saucepan, warm the cream over medium heat.
Spoon over the shells, and sprinkle with the remaining Parmesan.
Cover and bake until the sauce is bubbling, about 25 minutes.
Remove the cover and set under a broiler until the top is golden brown, 2 to 3 minutes.

Serves about 4
This pairs well with roasted chicken or lamb.
For a complete meal, add another vegetable or salad.

ROASTED SQUASH WITH LEEK AND BARLEY PILAF

1 1/4 cup pearl barley
1 bay leaf
1 Kent pumpkin or buttercup squash or similar squash
1/4 cup olive oil, divided
Salt and pepper to taste
1 tablespoon small thyme sprigs, divided
1 to 2 pinches dried hot pepper flakes to taste
2 tablespoons butter, divided
2 to 3 celery ribs, sliced
4 leeks, thickly sliced
8 ounces brown mushrooms, sliced
2 carrots, coarsely shredded
1/2 to 3/4 cup vegetable stock
Handful of flat leaf parsley, roughly chopped
3 tablespoons lightly toasted pumpkin seeds, optional
6 to 8 ounces Taleggio or Fontina cheese, thinly sliced

Rinse barley well.
Put it into a large saucepan with the bay leaf.
Cover generously with water and bring to a boil.
Reduce heat and simmer gently, partially covered for 30 to 40 minutes until tender.
Drain and set aside until needed.
Preheat oven to 400*F.
Cut squash into 4 to 8 wedges.
Do not peel them but scoop out seeds.
Rub with half the oil and put on a baking sheet.
Season with salt and pepper and scatter over them with half the thyme and hot pepper flakes.
Roast, uncovered, in the preheated oven for about 40 minutes or until tender and browned.
Meanwhile heat remains oil and half the butt in a large skillet.
Cook celery gently for 5 minutes.
Add leeks and most of remaining thyme.
Cook for another 4 to 5 minutes, stirring once or twice.
Add mushrooms and cook for 1 to 2 minutes more.
Add barley and stir, adding sufficient stock to make grains moist and reheat thoroughly.
Check seasonings and stir in parsley, pumpkin seeds and remaining butter.
To serve; top squash with pilaf mixture and sliced cheese and remaining few thyme sprigs.
Sprinkle with pepper and let cheese melt under hot broiler until it bubbles.
Serve immediately with any additional pilaf.
Yield: Serves 4.

ROSEMARY CRANBERRY BUTTERNUT SQUASH SIDE DISH WITH QUINOA

1 butternut squash
1/2 cup of honey
1 cup dried cranberries
1/2 cup quinoa
1/2 cup water
2 teaspoons of fresh minced rosemary + more decoration

Combine quinoa and water in a small saucepan, cover, bring to a boil, reduce heat and simmer until water is absorbed, about 15 minutes.
Meanwhile, preheat the oven to 375*F.
Peel and dice the butternut squash into 1-inch cubes.
Place the butternut squash, cranberries, honey, quinoa and rosemary into a large mixing bowl; combine until thoroughly coated, then transfer to a baking dish.
Cover and bake for 1 hour.

Yield: Serves 4

Butternut squash is called butternut pumpkin in Australia and other parts of the world. It is probably one of the most popular squashes.

STUFFED PUMPKIN BLOSSOMS
Pumpkin Blossoms
Your Favorite Ground Beef, Pork Sausage, or Feta and Ricotta Cheese mixture,

Pick Blossoms just after they wilt (mid-morning)
Rinse in Clear Water, Lay on towel to absorb excess water
Fill with your favorite mixture.
Close petals over mixture, place side by side in greased baking dish.
Bake in moderate oven (330*F) about 15 minutes or until filling is heated through.
Cover to Keep blossoms moist.

our favorite Fillings to use are: Ricotta and Pumpkin (page 41) and any cooked ground meats seasoned with Italian seasonings.

SWEET AND SOUR SOUTH INDIAN PUMPKIN

1 tablespoon ground coriander
1 teaspoon chopped fresh ginger
2 cloves garlic, chopped fine
Pinch cayenne pepper or to taste
1/4 teaspoon ground black pepper
3 tablespoons canola oil
2 pounds pumpkin, peeled and cut
    into 1 1/2-inch pieces, about 6 cups
Salt
2 tablespoons lemon juice
3 tablespoons light brown sugar
1 tablespoon chopped cilantro

Preheat oven to 350 degrees F.

In a small bowl, combine the ground coriander, ginger, garlic, cayenne and black pepper.
Heat the oil in a large oven-proof pan over medium heat until hot.
Add the spice mixture and cook stirring until it turns a little darker and is very aromatic, about 1 minute.
Do not burn!
Immediately add the pumpkin and stir to coat with the spices.
Sprinkle with about 1/2 teaspoon salt and cover.
Set in the oven and bake until the pumpkin is just barely tender, about 25 minutes.
Remove the pan from the oven.
Using a slotted spoon, remove the pumpkin pieces.
Set the pan over medium-high heat, stir in the lemon juice, and cook, uncovered for 1 minute.
Stir in the brown sugar and cook 3 to 4 minutes until the sugar dissolves and he juices are syrupy.
Add the pumpkin and toss.
Season with more salt and pepper to taste.
Sprinkle with the fresh coriander and serve.

Yield: Serves 6
Tip: Use three or four different varieties of Pumpkin or Squash for a standout dish
    recommended: Kent, Jarrahdale, Moranga, Long Island Cheese or Hubbard (any)

CURRIED BUTTERNUT SQUASH KABOBS

Fix these ahead of time and have them ready to go.

1 butternut squash, peeled and cut into 1-inch cubes
3 tablespoons butter, melted
1 teaspoon curry powder
1/4 teaspoon salt

Place squash in a greased 9 x 13 baking dish.
Combine the butter, curry powder and salt; drizzle over squash and toss to coat.
Bake, uncovered, at 450 degrees F for 20-25 minutes or until tender and lightly browned stirring twice.
Cool on a wire rack.
Thread squash cubes onto 12 metal or soaked wooden skewers.
Grill, covered, over medium heat for 3-5 minutes on each side or until heated through.

PUMPKIN PASTA SAUCE

1 cup freshly grated Parmesan cheese, divided
1 pound rotini, cooked
1/4 cup butter or margarine
1 leek, diced
1 celery rib, diced
3 pounds peeled pumpkin (squash), chopped
1-14 1/2 ounce can chicken broth
1/2 teaspoon salt
1/2 teaspoon pepper
1/4 teaspoon ground nutmeg
2/3 cup heavy cream

Toss 1/2 cup Parmesan cheese with pasta, and keep warm.
Melt butter in a large saucepan over medium heat; add leek and celery, and sauté until tender.
Add pumpkin; sauté 2 to 3 minutes.
Add broth; bring to a boil.
Cover and reduce heat, simmer for 20 minutes.
Add salt, pepper and nutmeg.
Process pumpkin mixture in a blender until smooth.
Return to saucepan, stir in cream, and cook over low heat, stirring often, until heated.
Serve over pasta; top with remaining cheese.

Yield: 6 servings.

PUMPKIN FRITTERS

3 eggs, separated
½ tsp salt
Dash of pepper
2 Tbs flour
1 cup cooked pumpkin
1 inch oil in skillet

Beat together egg yolks, salt, pepper, flour and pumpkin.
Beat egg whites until stiff and fold gently into mixture.
Drop by spoonful into hot oil and fry until browned on one side.
Turn and fry other side.
Drain on paper towels.
Serve with honey.

Yield: 2 Servings

PUMPKIN CURLS

Honeynut Squash Pumpkin
Vegetable Peeler
Cast Iron Fry Pan
Oil, Salt

Wash pumpkin well, remove stem.
Heat fry pan with a dash of oil.
Peel pumpkin directly into hot pan the desired amount.
Stir gently for 3 minutes or until translucent and crispy. Add salt and pepper to taste.

This is a great addition for burgers, sloppy joes, hot wraps as well as breakfast with eggs and hashbrowns.

SAUTÉED PUMPKIN BLOSSOMS

2 cups pumpkin blossoms, partially opened
2 Tbs butter
½ teas salt
Dash of pepper

Heat butter in a crepe pan or electric skillet
Add the washed and dried pumpkin blossoms.
Turn them gently in the skillet for 2-3 minutes.
Most will burst into full blossom in the heat.
Do not brown.
Sprinkle with salt and pepper.
Serve at once.

Serves 3-4 persons.

May be prepared at the table before guests as it is exciting to watch the blossoms burst open.

SQUASH PATTIES

3 cups shredded butternut squash
1 small onion, minced
3/4 cup cornmeal
1/4 cup flour
1/2 teaspoon salt
1/4 teaspoon pepper
1/8 teaspoon ground red pepper
1/2 cup milk
1 large egg
Vegetable oil
Addition sea salt if desired

Combine squash and onion.
Mix the next 5 ingredients and add to the squash mixture.
Beat the egg, add the milk; add to the squash and flour mixture.
Heat 1/4-to-1/2-inch oil in a frying pan.
Form mixture into 1/2 inch thick by 3 inches across patties, fry 3-5 minutes or until browned on each side.
Sprinkle with sea salt if desired and serve.

SWEETER SIDES

APPLE STUFFED ACORN SQUASH

1 large acorn squash, halved and seeded
1 cup water
3 tablespoons butter, melted
1/2 to 1 teaspoon lemon juice
1/2 teaspoon cinnamon
2 tablespoons brown sugar, firmly packed
1 large Granny Smith apple, peeled, cored, and chopped
1/4 cup chopped nuts of your choice, optional

Heat oven to 350*F.
Place squash cut side down, in a large baking pan or dish; pour water into bottom of pan around the squash.
Bake 20 minutes.
Remove from oven.
Meanwhile, in a bowl, combine butter, lemon juice, cinnamon, brown sugar, and chopped apples.
Divide mixture evenly among partially cooked squash and return to oven for 30 minutes or until tender when flesh is poked with a fork.
Sprinkle with chopped nuts to serve.

Yield: 2 servings

Variations: mix in some blueberries, fresh or frozen or cranberries, fresh, frozen, or dried.

BAKED ACORN SQUASH

1 acorn squash, halved
2 tablespoons butter
2 teaspoons honey or maple syrup
2 tablespoons firmly packed brown sugar
Salt and pepper to taste

Preheat oven to 375*F.
Cut squash in half lengthwise and remove fibers and seeds.
Add 1 tablespoon of butter, 1 teaspoon of honey or maple syrup, 1 tablespoon of brown sugar, salt and pepper to the hollow scoop of each squash half.
Place upright on a greased cookie sheet and roast for 20-30 minutes or until tender when flesh is poked with a fork.

Yield: 2 serving

Carnival, Festival, and Sweet Dumpling squashes can all be used in any recipe that call for Acorn squash.

CINNAMON SQUASH RINGS

2 tablespoons packed brown sugar
2 tablespoons milk
1 egg
3/4 cup soft bread crumbs
1/4 cup yellow or white cornmeal
2 teaspoons ground cinnamon
1 large acorn squash, seeded, and cut crosswise into 1/2-inch slices
1/3 cup butter, melted

Preheat oven to 400 degrees F.
Mix brown sugar, milk and egg.
Mix bread crumbs, cornmeal and cinnamon.
Dip squash slices into egg mixture, then coat with bread crumb mixture; repeat one more.
Place squash slices in an untreated 9x13 inch baking pan.
Drizzle with butter, and bake uncovered until squash is tender, about 35 minutes.

Other Types: North Georgia Candy Roaster, Delicata

LEMONY SQUASH SLICES

2 LARGE ACORN, CARNIVAL OR SWEET DUMPLING SQUASH
1 CUP PLUS 2 TABLESPOONS WATER, DIVIDED
1/2 CUP SUGAR
2 TABLESPOONS LEMON JUICE
1 TABLESPOON BUTTER
1/4 TEASPOON SALT
1/8 TEASPOON PEPPER
LEMON WEDGES AND FRESH MINT (OPTIONAL)

Cut squash in half lengthwise; remove and discard the seeds and membranes.
Cut each half crosswise into 1/2-inch slices.
Place slices in a large skillet; add 1 cup water; bring to a boil.
Reduce heat; cover and simmer for 20 minutes or until tender.
Meanwhile, in a heavy saucepan, combine sugar and remaining water.
Cook over medium heat until sugar melts and syrup is golden, stirring occasionally.
Remove from the heat; carefully add the lemon juice, butter, salt and pepper.
Cook and stir over low heat until butter melts.
Place squash on a serving plate; top with syrup.
Garnish with lemon and mint if desired.

YIELD: 6 SERVING.

MAPLE BUTTERNUT SQUASH

1 MEDIUM BUTTERNUT SQUASH, SEEDED, PEELED AND CUBED
1/2 CUP MAPLE SYRUP
2 TABLESPOONS RAISINS OR CRANBERRIES
1 TABLESPOON BUTTER, MELTED
1/2 TEASPOON CARDAMOM
1/2 TEASPOON GROUND ALLSPICE

Preheat oven to 350*F
In a small bowl, combine the syrup, raisins, butter and spices; set aside.
Place in a 9 x 13-inch baking pan.
Drizzle with syrup mixture.
Cover and bake for 20 minutes.
Uncover, bake 15 minutes longer or until squash is tender.

YIELD: 6 SERVING.

ACORN SQUASH FETA CASSEROLE

2 large acorn squash
1 medium onion, chopped
2 garlic cloves, minced
3 tablespoons butter or margarine
1/2 cup chopped green pepper
1/2 cup chopped sweet red pepper
2 eggs
1 cup plain yogurt
1 cup crumbled feta cheese
1 teaspoon salt
1/2 teaspoon pepper
Dash cayenne pepper, optional
1/4 cup sunflower kernels

Cut squash in half; discard insides and seeds.
Place squash cut side down in a large greased baking pan.
Bake at 350 degrees F for 45-50 minutes or until tender; cool slightly.
Carefully scoop out squash; place in a bowl and mash.
In a skillet, sauté onion and garlic in butter until tender.
Add peppers; sauté until crisp-tender.
In a large bowl, whisk eggs and yogurt until blended.
Stir in squash, onion mixture, feta cheese, salt, pepper and cayenne pepper.
Transfer to a greased 7 x 11 x 2-inch baking dish.
Sprinkle with sunflower kernels.
Cover and bake at 375 degrees F for 25 minutes or until a knife inserted near the center comes out clean.

Yield: 6-8 servings.

Try other varieties of squash in this recipe.

BUTTERNUT BARLEY RISOTTO

1 butternut squash, peeled and cubed, about 3 lbs
2 tablespoons olive oil
1 medium leek, chopped fine
1 clove garlic, crushed
1 1/2 cups pearl barley, rinsed
1/2 dry white wine
3 cups vegetable or chicken stock
3 cups water
6 leaves Swiss chard, shredded finely
1 cup frozen peas, thawed
2/3 cup grated Parmesan cheese

Boil, steam or microwave butternut squash until tender; drain.
Mash two-thirds of squash; reserve remaining pieces.
Heat oil in a large saucepan; cook leek and garlic, stirring, until leek is soft.
Add barley; stir until combined.
Add wine; simmer, uncovered, until almost all wine is evaporated.
Stir in stock and the water; simmer, uncovered, about 40 minutes or until barley is tender, stirring occasionally.
Add Swiss chard; stir until wilted.
Add mashed squash, reserved squash pieces, peas and cheese;
stir until heated through.
Best made close to serving.

Yield: Serves 4
Variation: Top with chopped ham or chicken.

BUTTERNUT SQUASH PUFF

2 cups hot mashed butternut squash, or squash or pumpkin of your choice
3 eggs, separated
1/4 cup flour
1/4 cup minced parsley
2 tablespoons butter or margarine
2 teaspoons finely chopped onion
2 teaspoons lemon juice
1/2 teaspoon dried thyme
1/4 teaspoon salt
1/2-pound bulk pork sausage, cooked and drained
Fresh thyme, optional

In a bowl, combine squash, egg yolks, flour, parsley, butter, onion, lemon juice, thyme, and salt; mix until well blended.
Stir in sausage.
Cool for 10 minutes.
In a small mixing bowl, beat egg whites until stiff peaks form; fold into squash mixture.
Pour into a greased and floured 2-quart baking dish.
Bake, uncovered, at 375*F for 45-50 minutes or until a knife inserted near the center comes out clean.
Garnish with thyme if desired.

Yield: 4-6 servings.

CURRIED BEEF STUFFED SQUASH

3 medium acorn squash, halved and seeded
1 pound ground beef
1/2 cup chopped onion
2 garlic cloves, minced
1 teaspoon beef bouillon granules
1/2 cup hot water
1/2 cup cooked rice
2 tablespoons chopped fresh parsley
1 tablespoon orange concentrate
1 teaspoon brown sugar
1 teaspoon curry powder
1/2 teaspoon ground ginger
1/4 teaspoon salt.

Invert squash on a greased 10 x 15 x 1 inch baking pan.
Bake, uncovered, at 350 degrees F for 35-45 minutes or until almost tender.
Meanwhile, in a skillet, cook beef, onion and garlic until meat is browned and onion is tender; drain.
Dissolve bouillon in water; add to skillet.
Stir in remaining ingredients; mix well.
Turn squash cut side up in pan and fill with meat mixture.
Fill pan with hot water to a depth of 1/4 inch, cover loosely with foil.
Bake at 350 degrees F for 20-30 minutes or until heated through.

Yield: 6 servings

EASY SPAGHETTI SQUASH BOATS

2 MINI SPAGHETTI SQUASH
1/2-POUND GROUND BEEF
1/2 CUP CHOPPED ONION
1/2 CUP CHOPPED SWEET PEPPER
1 CLOVE GARLIC, MINCED
1/2 TEASPOON BASIL
1/2 TEASPOON DRIED OREGANO
1/4 TEASPOON PEPPER
1 CAN (14 1/2 OUNCES) PETITE DICED TOMATOES
 OR EQUIVALENT AMOUNT OF FRESH DICED TOMATOES
1/3 CUP MOZZARELLA CHEESE, SHREDDED

Preheat oven to 375*F
Cut squash in half lengthwise; scoop out seeds.
Place squash, cut side down, in a baking dish.
Bake, uncovered, for 30-40 minutes or until tender.
Meanwhile, in a skillet over medium heat, cook beef, onions and sweet peppers until meat is browned and vegetables are tender; drain fat.
Add garlic, basil, oregano, salt and pepper; cook and stir for 2 minutes.
Add tomatoes; cook and stir for 2 minutes.
Remove spaghetti halves from oven, turn over and fill with sauce mixture.
Sprinkle with cheese and return to oven for about 10 minutes or until cheese is melted.
Serve the spaghetti boats in the shell.
Use a fork to pull some of the strands with the sauce to eat.

YIELD: 4 SIDE DISH SERVINGS OR 2 MAIN DISH SERVINGS.

OPTIONAL: ADD MUSHROOMS TO THE SAUCE MIXTURE. AND/OR A SMALL AMOUNT OF YOUR FAVORITE SPICY PEPPER.

VEGETARIAN: OMIT THE GROUND BEEF.

HUBBARD SQUASH MEAL

1 medium Hubbard squash
2 pounds hamburger
2 boxes of Zatarain Dirty Rice
28 ounce can stewed tomatoes
2 cups water
1 cup beef broth
1 teaspoon salt (optional)
Melted butter
Pepper

Cut a hole in the top of the squash (like you would to carve a pumpkin), remove seeds and stringy pulp. Set on heavy cooking sheet.
Brush with and sprinkle with salt and pepper.
In a large Dutch oven or similar pot, brown the hamburger, add the rest of the ingredients.
Bring to a simmer; when liquid is absorbed put mixture into the squash.
Return the top.
Bake the squash in a 350-degree oven for 15 minutes for each pound of the squash.
Example a 10-pound squash will take approximately 2 1/2 hours.

Yield: Serves 8-10

SPAGHETTI SQUASH ALFREDO

1 MEDIUM SPAGHETTI SQUASH, COOKED BY YOUR FAVORITE METHOD AND SEPARATED INTO STRANDS
1 CUP SOUR CREAM
1/2 CUP SHREDDED MOZZARELLA CHEESE
1/4 CUP GRATED PARMESAN CHEESE
2 CLOVES GARLIC, FINELY MINCED
1/4 TEASPOON SALT
1/4 TEASPOON PEPPER

In a medium saucepan, combine all ingredients except spaghetti squash over a medium-low heat and whisk until smooth and creamy, stirring constantly to prevent burning.
Add the spaghetti squash strands to the sauce and stir until thoroughly mixed and heated through.
Serve immediately.

SERVES 6 TO 8

SPAGHETTI SQUASH, ITALIAN STYLE

1 small spaghetti squash
1 small onion
6 to 8 large fresh basil leaves or 1 teaspoon dried crushed basil leaves
2 tablespoons olive oil
2 ripe tomatoes, cored and chopped
Salt and pepper to taste
Grated Parmesan cheese

Preheat oven to 350 degrees F.
Cut squash in half, remove seeds and place spaghetti squash on cookie sheet and bake it oven for 1 hour, or until flesh is just tender.
Meanwhile, peel and chop onion.
Mince basil leaves.
Heat olive oil in medium skillet.
Add onion and basil, sauté 5 minutes.
Add tomatoes and simmer another 10 minutes.
Season to taste with salt and pepper.
Remove from heat and set aside.
Using a fork separate the spaghetti-like strands from the spaghetti squash.
Spoon spaghetti squash into skillet with tomatoes sauce.
Toss over moderate heat briefing to heat through. T
taste and adjust seasonings, if necessary.
Sprinkle about 2 tablespoons grated Parmesan cheese on each helping as serving.

Yield: 2 Servings

Also can add diced peppers to the sauce.

SPAGHETTI SQUASH SALAD

1 spaghetti squash about 2 1/2 pounds
1 large onion, finely chopped
1 cup sugar
1 cup diced celery
1/2 cup chopped sweet red pepper
1/2 cup chopped green pepper
1/2 cup vegetable oil
1/4 cup vinegar
1/2 teaspoon salt

Cut squash in half lengthwise; scoop out seeds.
Place squash, cut side down, in a baking dish.
Bake uncovered, at 375 degrees F for 30-40 minutes or until tender.
When cool enough to handle, scoop out the squash, separating strands with a fork.
Combine remaining ingredients in a bowl; add squash and stir well.
Cover and refrigerate for at least 2 hours.
Serve with a slotted spoon as a salad or as a relish with burgers and hot dogs.
Store in the refrigerator.

Yield: 8 servings

STUFFED SQUASH

1 3-pound turban squash
2 tablespoons butter
1/4 cup chopped yellow onion
1 rib celery, chopped
1 fresh carrot, finely diced
1/2-pound pork sausage

1/4 cup bread crumbs
2 tablespoons light brown sugar
1 teaspoon salt
1/2 teaspoon black pepper

Preheat oven to 350 degrees F.
Grease a baking sheet.
Cut top off turban squash; set aside.
Scoop out seeds; discard.
Place squash cut-side down on prepared baking sheet.
Cover with baking foil.
Bake until tender, about 50-60 minutes.
Remove from oven.
Scoop pulp from cavity; set aside.
Heat butter in a nonstick saucepan.
Add onion, celery, carrot and sausage; cook and stir over medium heat until vegetables are tender and sausage is browned; drain and discard fat.
Stir in bread crumbs, sugar, salt, pepper and cooked squash pulp.
Spoon filling into cavity of squash.
Cover with the top that was set aside.
Bake until heated through, about 25 minutes.

Serve hot. Refrigerate leftovers.

Yield: 4 servings.

Other Varieties: Butterkin, Autumn Frost, Kent, Strawberry Crown, Tekasukabuto, Black Futsu

CHEWY PUMPKIN BARS WITH CARAMEL DRIZZLE

2 CUPS FLOUR
1 1/2 TEASPOONS BAKING POWDER
1 TEASPOON BAKING SODA
1/2 TEASPOON SALT
2 TEASPOONS GROUND CINNAMON
1 TEASPOON GROUND GINGER
1/2 TEASPOON GRATED NUTMEG
1/4 TEASPOON GROUND CLOVES
1 STICK BUTTER, SOFTENED
1 1/4 CUPS PACKED BROWN SUGAR
1 CUP PUMPKIN PURÉE
2 LARGE EGGS
1 CUP RAISINS OR DRIED CRANBERRIES
CARAMEL DRIZZLE (RECIPE FOLLOWS)

Preheat oven to 350* F.
Grease a 10x15 inch baking pan and line it with parchment paper.
Whisk together the flour, baking powder, baking soda, salt and spices in a large bowl.
Cream the butter and sugar until light and fluffy with an electric mixer.
Blend in the pumpkin and then the eggs, one at a time.
Slowly add the dry ingredients and the raisins or cranberries, beating until just blended.
Spread the batter thinly in the prepared pan and bake for 20 minutes or until a toothpick inserted near the middle comes out clean.
Cool completely before applying the caramel drizzle.

CARAMEL DRIZZLE
4 TABLESPOONS BUTTER
1/3 CUP PACKED LIGHT BROWN SUGAR
1 TEASPOON VANILLA
1 CUP CONFECTIONERS' SUGAR
3 TABLESPOONS HALF AND HALF

Melt the butter in a medium saucepan over low heat. Add the brown sugar and stir until dissolved; whisk in the vanilla, confectioners' sugar and half and half. Add a little more half and half if the consistency is too thick; if too thin add additional confectioners' sugar. Drizzle the caramel in a diagonal plaid pattern over the cooled bars. Cut into 1 x 3-inch bars.

These bars can be frozen.

CRUNCHY-TOPPED SPICE CAKE

3 EGGS
1/2 CUP BUTTER OR MARGARINE, MELTED
2 CUPS PUMPKIN PURÉE
1 PACKAGE (18 OZ) SPICE CAKE MIX
1 1/2 CUPS FINELY CHOPPED WALNUTS, DIVIDED
1 CUP BUTTERSCOTCH CHIPS

Preheat oven to 350*F
In a mixing bowl, combine the eggs, butter, and pumpkin.
Add cake mix, beat on medium speed for 2 minutes.
Stir in 3/4 cup walnuts.
Pour into a greased 9 x 13-inch cake pan.
Sprinkle with butterscotch chips and remaining nuts.
Bake 35-40 minutes or until a toothpick inserted near the center comes out clean.

YIELD: 12-15 SERVINGS.

PUMPKIN BARS

1 teaspoon baking soda
2 teaspoons baking powder
1/2 teaspoon salt
1 1/3 cup white sugar
4 eggs
1 cup nuts (optional)
1 cup oil
2 cups pumpkin purée
1 teaspoon vanilla
2 teaspoons cinnamon
1/2 teaspoons each ginger, cloves, allspice
2 cups flour

FROSTING:
4 ounces cream cheese
1/2 stick of butter or oleo
1 teaspoon vanilla
1 1/2 cup powdered sugar.

Preheat oven to 350*F
Sift flour, baking soda, baking powder, salt, and spices together.
Beat eggs, add sugar, oil, pumpkin, nuts and vanilla.
Add sifted ingredients and mix well.
Pour into greased jelly roll pan.
Bake for 25-30 minutes.
Cool on baking rack.
Combine frosting ingredients, beat until fluffy. Frost bars.

Variations: add 1 cup of raisins OR dried cranberries OR chocolate chips.

These are a Family favorite for every occasion.

PUMPKIN CAKE ROLL

CAKE:
4 eggs
1/2 cup honey
3/4 cup pumpkin purée
1 1/2 teaspoons lemon juice
1 cup flour
2 teaspoons baking powder
1 teaspoon baking soda
2 1/2 teaspoons cinnamon
1 teaspoon ginger

FILLING:
1 - 8-ounce package cream cheese
1 cup confectioners' sugar
1/4 cup butter or margarine
1/2 teaspoon vanilla
Additional sugar for dusting

Preheat oven to 350*F;
Grease and flour a 17x11x2 inch pan. (Hint: line the pan with parchment paper.)
In a large bowl, beat eggs until foamy and lemon colored, about 3 minutes.
Beat in honey, pumpkin, and lemon juice.
Sift together flour, baking powder, baking soda, cinnamon, and ginger into egg mixture.
Beat for about one minute.
Turn into prepared pan, and bake on middle shelf of oven for 10 to 15 minutes, or until cake springs back when pressed in the middle.
Immediately turn out on linen towel dusted with confectioners' sugar.
Roll up cake in towel, starting with short end.
Cool.
Meanwhile, in a mixing bowl, beat cream cheese, sugar, butter and vanilla until fluffy.
Carefully unroll cake.
Spread filling over cake to within 1 inch of edges.
Roll up again.
Cover and chill until serving.

Dust with sugar if desired.

CAN BE FROZEN

PUMPKIN CHIP COOKIES

1 1/2 cups butter
2 cups packed brown sugar
1 cup sugar
2 cups pumpkin purée
1 egg
1 teaspoon vanilla extract
4 cups flour
2 cups quick cooking oats
2 teaspoon baking soda
2 teaspoons ground cinnamon
1 teaspoon salt
2 cups semisweet chocolate chips.

Preheat oven to 350*F
In a large mixing bowl, cream bitter and sugars.
Beat in the pumpkin, egg and vanilla.
Combine the flour, oats, baking soda, cinnamon and salt; gradually add to creamed mixture.
Stir in chocolate chips.
Drop by tablespoons 2 inches apart onto untreated baking sheets.
Bake 10-13 minutes or until lightly browned.
Remove to wire racks to cool.

Yield 10 dozen.

PUMPKIN CHOCOLATE CHIP CAKE

1 cup less 2 tablespoons vegetable oil
2 cups sugar
2 eggs
2 cups pumpkin purée
1 cup nuts
1 cup chocolate chips
2 cups flour
1 teaspoon salt
2 teaspoons baking soda
2 teaspoons baking powder
1 teaspoon cinnamon
1 teaspoon vanilla

Sift together flour, salt, baking soda, baking powder, and cinnamon.
Mix oil, sugar, eggs, pumpkin purée, and vanilla.
Blend with dry ingredients, add chopped nuts and chocolate chips.
Pour into a 9 x 13-inch baking pan.
Bake at 350 degrees F for 25-30 minutes or until done.
Frost with cream cheese frosting or chocolate frosting.

Cake freezes well.

Cream cheese frosting:
4 ounces cream cheese
1/2 stick of butter or oleo
1 teaspoon vanilla
1 1/2 cup powdered sugar

Combine frosting ingredients and beat until fluffy.
Frost cake.

PUMPKIN POUND CAKE

1 cup butter or margarine, softened
3 cups sugar
5 eggs
3 cups flour
2 teaspoons baking powder
1/2 teaspoon baking soda
Salt
2 teaspoons cinnamon
1/2 teaspoon ground cloves
1/8 teaspoon nutmeg
2 cups pumpkin purée
1/3 cup rum

Preheat oven to 350*F
Beat butter at medium speed about 2 minutes or until light and creamy.
Gradually add sugar, beating at medium speed for 5-7 minutes.
Add eggs, one at a time, beating until yellow disappears.
Combine flour, baking powder, soda, salt and spices.
Combine pumpkin and rum.
Add flour mixture to creamed mixture, alternating with pumpkin mixture, beginning and ending with flour mixture.
After each addition, mix at lowest speed until just blended.
Pour into a greased and floured tube pan.
Bake for 1 hour and 25-30 minutes.
Cool on wire rack.
Remove from pan.

May wrap with plastic wrap when still warm.

PUMPKIN SPICE CAKE

1/4 cup butter, softened
1/2 cup packed brown sugar
2 Tablespoons sugar
1 1/2 teaspoons grated orange peel
3 egg whites
1 cup pumpkin purée
1/4 cup light corn syrup
2 Tablespoon molasses
1 1/4 cup flour
1 teaspoon baking soda
1/2 teaspoon ground cinnamon
1/2 teaspoon ground ginger
1/4 teaspoon salt
Whipped cream, optional

Preheat oven to 350*F
In a large mixing bowl, cream the butter, sugars and the orange peel.
Add egg whites, one at a time, beating well after each addition.
Beat the pumpkin, corn syrup and molasses until blended.
Combine the flour, baking soda, baking powder, cinnamon, ginger and salt; add to pumpkin mixture, beating on low speed just until moistened.
Pour into a greased 8-inch baking dish.
Bake for 30-35 minutes or until a toothpick inserted near the center comes out clean.
Cool on a wire rack for 15 minutes.
Serve warm with whipped cream if desired.

Yield: 9 serving.

This cake is similar to a gingerbread cake.

LIGHT-TEXTURED PUMPKIN PIE

2 cups cooked pumpkin
4 eggs, separated
1 cup sugar
1 Tbs cornstarch
½ tsp cinnamon
1/3 cup cream
¼ cup butter, melted
1 9-inch unbaked pie shell

Preheat oven to 375*F
Combine pumpkin, slightly beaten egg yolks and mixture of sugar, cornstarch and cinnamon.
Beat 5 minutes.
Mix in cream and butter.
Beat egg whites until rounded peaks form and fold into pumpkin mixture.
Pour into pie shell and bake 45 minutes or until inserted knife comes out clean.

PUMPKIN CHEESECAKE WITH SOUR CREAM TOPPING

CRUST:
1 1/2 cups graham cracker crumbs
1/4 cup sugar
1/3 cup butter or margarine, melted

FILLING:
3 packages (8 ounces each) cream cheese, softened
1 cup brown sugar
2 cups pumpkin purée
2 tablespoons cornstarch
1 1/2 teaspoons ground cinnamon
1/2 teaspoon ground nutmeg
1 can (5 ounce) evaporated milk
2 eggs

TOPPING:
2 cups sour cream
1/3 cup sugar
1 teaspoon vanilla extract
Additional ground cinnamon, optional

Preheat oven to 350*F
In a bowl, combine crumbs and sugar; stir in butter.
Press onto the bottom and 1 1/2 inches up the sides of a greased 9-inch springform pan.
Bake for 5 to 7 minutes or until set. Cool for 10 minutes.
In a mixing bowl, beat cream cheese and brown sugar until smooth.
Add the pumpkin, cornstarch, cinnamon and nutmeg; mix well.
Gradually beat in milk and eggs until just blended.
Pour into crust.
Bake for 55-60 minutes or until center is almost set.
Combine the sour cream, sugar and vanilla; spread over filling.
Bake 5 minutes longer.
Cool on a wire rack for 10 minutes.
Carefully run a knife around edge of pan to loosen; cool 1 hour longer.
Chill overnight.
Remove the sides of pan; let stand at room temperature for 30 minutes before slicing.
Sprinkle with cinnamon, if desired.
Refrigerate leftovers.

PUMPKIN CHIFFON PIE

1 ENVELOPE UNFLAVORED GELATIN
¼ CUP COLD WATER
1 ½ CUPS COOKED PUMPKIN
1 TSP GRATED LIME PEEL
¼ CUP LIME JUICE
10 TBS SUGAR
3 EGG WHITES
½ CUP WHIPPING CREAM
1 CUP TOASTED ALMONDS, SLICED
9" PIE SHELL BAKED

Soften gelatin in cold water for 5 minutes.
Be sure to completely dissolve by placing over simmering water.
Combine in separate bowl, the pumpkin, lime peel and juice, and 4 Tbs of the sugar.
Add gelatin, mix well, then chill until begins to thicken.
Beat egg whites until frothy, then beat in remaining 6 Tbs sugar one spoon at a time.
Beat until stiff but moist peaks form.
Fold in egg whites and ½ cup of the whipping cream, whipped, into the pumpkin mixture.
Pour into 9-inch pre-baked pie shell and chill until firm, about 3 hours.

PUMPKIN CREAM CHEESE PIE

CREAM CHEESE LAYER:
1 - 8-ounce package cream cheese, softened
1/4 cup sugar
1/2 teaspoon vanilla
1 slightly beaten egg

PUMPKIN LAYER:
1 1/4 cups pumpkin purée
1 cup evaporated milk
2 beaten eggs
1/4 cup sugar
1/4 cup brown sugar
1 teaspoon ground cinnamon
1/4 teaspoon salt
1/4 teaspoon nutmeg

TOPPING:
1/2 cup chopped pecans
2 tablespoons flour
2 tablespoons brown sugar
1 tablespoon butter, softened

1 unbaked pie shell

Preheat oven to 350*F
In a small mixing bowl, beat the cream cheese, 1/4 cup granulated sugar, vanilla, and the egg until smooth.
Spoon into unbaked pie shell.
Combine pumpkin, evaporated milk, eggs, 1/4 sugar and 1/4 cup brown sugar, cinnamon, salt and nutmeg.
Carefully pour over cream cheese mixture.
Bake for 50 minutes.
Meanwhile, combine the pecans, flour, 2 tablespoons brown sugar, and butter.
Sprinkle over the pie.
Bake for 10 to 15 minutes more or until a knife inserted near the center comes clean.
Cool for 1 to 2 hours on a wire rack.

Refrigerate, cover for longer storage.

PUMPKIN FUDGE

3 CUPS SUGAR
3/4 CUP MELTED BUTTER
2/3 CUP EVAPORATED MILK
1/2 CUP PUMPKIN PURÉE
2 TABLESPOONS CORN SYRUP
1 TEASPOON PUMPKINS PIE SPICE
1–12-OUNCE PACKAGE WHITE CHOCOLATE MORSELS
1–7-OUNCE JAR MARSHMALLOW CREME
1 CUP CHOPPED PECANS, TOASTED
1 TEASPOON VANILLA EXTRACT

Stir together first 6 ingredients in a 3 1/2-quart saucepan over medium-high heat, cook, stirring constantly, until mixture comes to a boil.
Cook, stirring constantly, until a candy thermometer registers 234 degrees (soft-ball stage) or about 12 minutes.
Remove pan from heat,
Stir in remaining ingredients until well blended.
Pour into a greased aluminum foil lined 9- inch square pan.
Let stand 2 hours or until completely cool; cut into squares.

YIELD: 3 POUNDS

PAGE 83

PUMPKIN MOUSSE

1 cup pumpkin purée
1/2 cup plain Greek yogurt
1/2 cup maple syrup
1/4 cup orange juice
1 envelope gelatin
1/4 cup whipping cream, very cold
Zest of one orange
1/2 teaspoon pumpkin pie spice

Put medium bowl in freezer.
In a large bowl, mix pumpkin and yogurt, using a whisk.
Sprinkle gelatin on orange juice and let sit for about three minutes, just enough time to get maple syrup ready.
Bring maple syrup to a boil on medium-high heat in a small saucepan, stirring constantly.
Pour boiling maple syrup over orange juice and stir until gelatin has melted.
Pour maple syrup mix into pumpkin mixture and mix well, using a whisk.
Add orange zest and spices; stir to combine.
In the chilled bowl from freezer, whip cream to firm peaks, using a hand mixer.
Use the mixer to whip the pumpkin mixture for about one minute.
Fold whipped cream gently into pumpkin mix using a spatula.
Ladle into serving cups and chill in the refrigerator for two to three hours, until set.

Yield: 4 servings

PUMPKIN PIE

1 1/2 cups pumpkin purée
3/4 cup sugar
1/2 teaspoon salt
1 to 1/2 teaspoons cinnamon
1/2 to 1 teaspoon ginger
1/4 to 1/2 teaspoon nutmeg
1/4 to 1/2 teaspoon cloves
3 slightly beaten eggs
1 1/4 cups milk
1 - 6 ounce can (2/3 cup) evaporated milk
1 - 9-inch unbaked pastry shell

Preheat oven to 400*F
Combine pumpkin, sugar, salt and spices.
Blend in eggs, milk and evaporated milk.
Pour into pastry shell (have edges crimped high because the amount of filling is generous).
Bake for 50 minutes or until knife inserted halfway between center and edge comes out clean.
Cool.

PUMPKIN PIE CUSTARD

1 cup pumpkin purée
1 can (12 ounces) fat free evaporated milk
8 egg whites
1/2 cup fat-free milk
3/4 cup sugar
1 teaspoon ground cinnamon
1/2 teaspoon ground ginger
1/4 teaspoon salt
1/4 teaspoon ground cloves
1/4 teaspoon ground nutmeg
Fat-free whipped topping, optional

Preheat oven to 350*F
In a large mixing bowl, beat pumpkin, evaporated milk eggs whites and fat-free milk until smooth.
Add sugar, cinnamon, ginger, salt, cloves, and nutmeg; mix well.
Spoon into 10 6-ounce ramekins or custard cups coated with nonstick cooking spray.
Place in a 15 x 10 x 1 inch baking pan.
Bake for 40-45 minutes or until a knife inserted near the center comes out clean.
Cook on a wire rack.
Refrigerate until serving.
Garnish with whipped topping if desired.

Yield: 10 servings

DRINKS
9   Pumpkin Pie Smoothie

SNACKS

7   Honey Orange Ginger Pumpkin Butter
7   Pumpkin Cheese Ball
8   Pumpkin Harvest Dip
8   Pumpkin Hummus
10   How to prepare seeds
11   Roasted Pumpkin Seeds
11   Spicy Pumpkin Seeds

BREAKFAST AND BREADS
15   Frosted Pumpkin Doughnuts
16   Oatmeal Pumpkin Bread
17   Pumpkin Bread
18   Pumpkin Chip Muffins
19   Pumpkin Corn Bread
20   Pumpkin Muffins
21   Pumpkin Pancakes
22   Ribbon Pumpkin Bread

YEAST BREADS
23   Buttercup Squash Bread
24   Pumpkin Knot Rolls
25   Pumpkin-Raisin Bread
26   Pumpkin Cinnamon Rolls

SOUP
29   Apple Pumpkin Soup
30   Bean and Squash Soup
31   Black Bean and Pumpkin Chili
32   Butternut Bisque
33   Corn and Squash Soup
34   Pumpkin Soup with Tortellini
35   Roasted Squash Soup
36   Turkey Butternut Squash Soup
37   Pumpkin Soup

SQUASH SIDE DISHES

SAVORY
- 41 Conchiglie Stuffed with Ricotta and Pumpkin
- 42 Roasted Squash with Leek and Barley Pilaf
- 43 Rosemary Cranberry Butternut Squash w/Quinoa
- 43 Stuffed Pumpkin Blossoms
- 44 Sweet and Sour South Indian Pumpkin
- 45 Curried Butternut Squash Kabobs
- 46 Pumpkin Pasta Sauce
- 47 Pumpkin Fritters
- 48 Sautéed Pumpkin Blossoms
- 48 Squash Patties
- 47 Pumpkin Curls

SWEET
- 49 Apple Stuffed Acorn Squash
- 50 Baked Acorn Squash
- 50 Cinnamon Squash Rings
- 51 Lemony Squash Slices
- 51 Maple Butternut Squash

SQUASH MEALS
- 55 Acorn Squash Feta Casserole
- 56 Butternut Barley Risotto
- 57 Butternut Squash Puff
- 58 Curried Beef Stuffed Squash
- 59 Easy Spaghetti Squash Boats
- 60 Hubbard Squash Meal
- 61 Spaghetti Squash Alfredo
- 62 Spaghetti Squash, Italian Style
- 63 Spaghetti Squash Salad
- 64 Stuffed Squash

CAKES, COOKIES AND BARS

69	Chewy Pumpkin Bars with Caramel Drizzle
70	Crunchy-Topped Spice Cake
71	Pumpkin Bars
72	Pumpkin Cake Roll
73	Pumpkin Chip Cookies
74	Pumpkin Chocolate Chip Cake
75	Pumpkin Pound Cake
76	Pumpkin Spice Cake

PIES, CHEESECAKES AND DESSERTS

79	Light-Textured Pumpkin Pie
80	Pumpkin Cheesecake w/Sour Cream Topping
81	Pumpkin Chiffon Pie
82	Pumpkin Cream Cheese Pie
83	Pumpkin Fudge
84	Pumpkin Mousse
85	Pumpkin Pie
86	Pumpkin Pie Custard

INDEX BY TYPES OF PUMPKIN AND SQUASH USED IN RECIPES

Acorn, All types, includes sweet dumpling

44	Sweet and Sour South Indian Pumpkin
48	Squash Patties
49	Apple Stuffed Acorn Squash
50	Baked Acorn Squash
50	Cinnamon Squash Rings
51	Lemony Squash Slices
55	Acorn Squash Feta Casserole
58	Curried Beef Stuffed Squash
64	Stuffed Squash

Buttercup, includes Kabocha styles, Black Futsu, Tekasukabuto

23	Buttercup Squash Bread
42	Roasted Squash w/leek and Barley Pilaf
44	Sweet and Sour South Indian Pumpkin
55	Acorn Squash Feta Casserole
64	Stuffed Squash

Butternut (All Types)

30	Bean and Squash Soup
32	Butternut Bisque
35	Roasted Squash Soup
36	Turkey Butternut Squash Soup
43	Rosemary Cranberry Butternut w/Quinoa
44	Sweet and Sour South Indian Pumpkin
45	Curried Butternut Squash Kabobs
46	Pumpkin Pasta Sauce
47	Pumpkin Curls
48	Squash Patties
51	Maple Butternut Squash
56	Butternut Barley Risotto
64	Stuffed Squash

INDEX BY TYPES OF PUMPKIN AND SQUASH USED, CONTINUED

CINDERELLA

34	PUMPKIN SOUP W/ TORTELLINI
44	SWEET AND SOUR SOUTH INDIAN PUMPKIN
51	MAPLE BUTTERNUT SQUASH
55	ACORN SQUASH FETA CASSEROLE
60	HUBBARD SQUASH MEAL
64	STUFFED SQUASH

DELICATA

50	CINNAMON SQUASH RINGS
51	LEMONY SQUASH SLICES

FAIRYTALE

30	BEAN AND SQUASH SOUP
44	SWEET AND SOUR SOUTH INDIAN PUMPKIN
46	PUMPKIN PASTA SAUCE
51	MAPLE BUTTERNUT SQUASH
55	ACORN SQUASH FETA CASSEROLE
60	HUBBARD SQUASH MEAL

HUBBARD (ALL TYPES)

35	ROASTED SQUASH SOUP
44	SWEET AND SOUR SOUTH INDIAN PUMPKIN
46	PUMPKIN PASTA SAUCE
55	ACORN SQUASH FETA CASSEROLE
60	HUBBARD SQUASH MEAL

INDEX BY TYPES OF PUMPKIN AND SQUASH, CONTINUED

Jarrahdale, Queensland Blue

- 34 Pumpkin Soup w/Tortellini
- 37 Pumpkin Soup
- 44 Sweet and Sour South Indian Pumpkin
- 46 Pumpkin Pasta Sauce
- 55 Acorn Squash Feta Casserole

Kent

- 30 Bean and Squash Soup
- 35 Roasted Squash Soup
- 37 Pumpkin Soup
- 42 Roasted Squash w/Leek and Barley Pilaf
- 44 Sweet and Sour South Indian Pumpkin
- 46 Pumpkin Pasta Sauce
- 51 Maple Butternut Squash
- 64 Stuffed Squash

Long Island Cheese

- 44 Sweet and Sour South Indian Pumpkin
- 51 Maple Butternut Squash
- 60 Hubbard Squash Meal
- 64 Stuffed Squash

Moranga

- 44 Sweet and Sour South Indian Pumpkin
- 45 Curried Butternut Squash Kabobs
- 51 Lemony Squash Slices
- 55 Acorn Squash Feta Casserole
- 60 Hubbard Squash Meal
- 64 Stuffed Squash

INDEX BY TYPES OF PUMPKIN AND SQUASH, CONTINUED

North Georgia Candy Roaster (Banana Types)

- 50 Cinnamon Squash Rings
- 55 Acorn Squash Feta Casserole

Peanut Shell Pumpkin

- 51 Lemony Squash Slices
- 55 Acorn Squash Feta Casserole
- 60 Hubbard Squash Meal

Pie Pumpkin, Sugar or Winter Luxury

- 25 Pumpkin-Raisin Yeast Bread
- 31 Black Bean and Pumpkin Chili
- 33 Corn and Squash Soup
- 47 Pumpkin Fritters
- 57 Butternut Squash Puff
- 51 Lemony Squash Slices
- 55 Acorn Squash Feta Casserole
- 64 Stuffed Squash

Desserts

- 69 Chewy Pumpkin Bars with Caramel Drizzle
- 70 Crunchy Topped Spice Cake
- 71 Pumpkin Bars
- 72 Pumpkin Cake Roll
- 73 Pumpkin Chip Cookies
- 74 Pumpkin Chocolate Chip Cake
- 75 Pumpkin Pound Cake
- 76 Pumpkin Spice Cake
- 79 Light Textured Pumpkin Pie
- 80 Pumpkin Cheesecake with Sour Cream Topping
- 81 Pumpkin Chiffon Pie
- 82 Pumpkin Cream Cheese Pie
- 83 Pumpkin Fudge
- 84 Pumpkin Mousse
- 85 Pumpkin Pie
- 86 Pumpkin Pie Custard

INDEX BY TYPES OF PUMPKIN AND SQUASH, CONTINUED

SPAGHETTI

59	EASY SPAGHETTI SQUASH BOATS
61	SPAGHETTI SQUASH ALFREDO
62	SPAGHETTI SQUASH, ITALIAN STYLE
63	SPAGHETTI SQUASH SALAD

TURBAN (ALL TYPES)

44	SWEET AND SOUR SOUTH INDIAN PUMPKIN
46	PUMPKIN PASTA SAUCE
64	STUFFED SQUASH

INDEX BY TYPE OF PUMPKIN, CONTINUED

Pumpkin Puree
> Any type of edible flesh from pumpkin or winter squash that has been cooked and blended smooth.   Canned pumpkin is an example.

- 7   Honey Orange Ginger Pumpkin Butter
- 7   Pumpkin Cheese Ball
- 8   Pumpkin Harvest Dip
- 8   Pumpkin Hummus
- 9   Pumpkin Pie Smoothie

Breakfast and Bread
- 15   Frosted Pumpkin Doughnuts
- 16   Oatmeal Pumpkin Bread
- 17   Pumpkin Bread
- 18   Pumpkin Chip Muffins
- 19   Pumpkin Corn Bread
- 20   Pumpkin Muffins
- 21   Pumpkin Pancakes
- 22   Ribbon Pumpkin Bread
- 24   Pumpkin Knot Rolls
- 26   Pumpkin Cinnamon Rolls

Soup
- 29   Apple Pumpkin Soup

Savory
- 41   Conchiglie Stuffed with Ricotta and Pumpkin

Desserts
- 69   Chewy Pumpkin Bars with Caramel Drizzle
- 70   Crunchy Topped Spice Cake
- 71   Pumpkin Bars
- 72   Pumpkin Cake Roll
- 73   Pumpkin Chip Cookies
- 74   Pumpkin Chocolate Chip Cake
- 75   Pumpkin Pound Cake
- 76   Pumpkin Spice Cake
- 79   Light Textured Pumpkin Pie
- 80   Pumpkin Cheesecake with Sour Cream Topping
- 82   Pumpkin Cream Cheese Pie
- 83   Pumpkin Fudge
- 84   Pumpkin Mousse
- 85   Pumpkin Pie
- 86   Pumpkin Pie Custard

INDEX BY TYPE OF PUMPKIN, CONTINUED

PUMPKIN, COOKED AND MASHED, ANY VARIETY

23	BUTTERCUP SQUASH BREAD
25	PUMPKIN-RAISIN YEAST BREAD
31	BLACK BEAN AND PUMPKIN CHILI
33	CORN AND SQUASH SOUP
37	PUMPKIN SOUP
47	PUMPKIN FRITTERS
57	BUTTERNUT SQUASH PUFF
81	PUMPKIN CHIFFON PIE

PUMPKIN SEEDS; ANY VARIETY

11	ROASTED PUMPKIN SEEDS
11	SPICY PUMPKIN SEEDS

PUMPKIN BLOSSOMS; ANY VARIETY

43	STUFFED PUMPKIN BLOSSOMS
48	SAUTÉED PUMPKIN BLOSSOMS

HOW TO ROAST, STORE, PUREE A PUMPKIN AND OTHER USEFUL TIPS

Pumpkin or (Winter Squash) is referenced many times in the previous pages, as an interchangeable word. These are the long storage varieties, with the exception of delicata. Delicata is classed as a winter squash even though the skin is thinner than the other types.

When a specific variety is mentioned, make the recipe using that kind for the first tasting. Try a different type of pumpkin (winter squash) for a complete flavor change!

All skin of the pumpkins are edible, although it is not reccommended other than Delicata and Kent. When scooping out cooked flesh, it is okay if a little skin inadvertently rides along.

Most pumpkins and winter squash will last for months when properly stored, allowing for cooking at a later time.
Pennie once had a Queensland Blue stored for a year! As a pumpkin is in storage, the sugars inside will develop, and sometimes increase the flavor. The skin may also change color. As long as the pumpkin does not have any soft spots or uneven discoloration showing, it will remain useful. Sometimes, you can cut out the 'bad' spot and use the rest of the pumpkin, as long as it still smells good.

DID YOU KNOW?
Pumpkin is a great source of fiber, potassium, vitamin A, vitamin C, antioxidents and is recognized as a low-GI food? Pumpkin is a super food!
The average Pumpkin or Winter Squash has a GI average of 51.

HOW TO PREPARE:
Wash and Scrub the outside of your pumpkin. Remove the stem, cut in half; remove seeds and fiber. Follow the Recipie as instructed.

TO ROAST IN MICROWAVE: Prepare as above, Cover with waxed paper or microwave safe lid; cook on HIGH for 6-10 minutes or until tender.
Season to taste.

This is also an excellent way to soften the pumpkins for ease of cutting. Start with 2 minutes on High if the flesh is too difficult to cut.

Microwave Ovens vary, adjust times as necessary.

AVERAGE YIELD OF A PUMPKIN:
A 4 pound pumpkin will be about 2 pounds trimmed
8 cups of chunks or grated will equal 4 cups cooked, pureed or drained pumpkin.

Some varieties vary as the flesh is denser, or thicker, resulting in a smaller seed cavity. These will yield higher than this average.

TO MAKE PUMPKIN PUREE:
Preheat Oven to 350*
Prepare Pumpkin by washing the outside and removing the stem.
Cut in half and remove seeds and fiber.
Place flesh down on a large baking sheet, bake for 45 minutes. Flesh should be transluscent with few little juice forming on tray
Remove from oven and let cool long enough to handle, about 20-25 minutes.
Scoop out the flesh into a large bowl.
Using Food processor, pulse for about 3-5 minutes or until pumpkin is desired smoothness.
Store in a covered container in the refrigerator for up to a week or freeze in 2 Cup airtight portions.

HOW TO MAKE PUMPKIN PIE SPICE:

3 Tablespoons Ground Cinnamon
2 Teaspoons Ground Ginger
1 teaspoon ground allspice
1 1/2 teaspoon ground nutmeg
1/2 teaspoon ground cloves.

Mix all the spices together in a small jar with lid. Use according to recipie or sprinkle on anything pumpkin.

www.ingramcontent.com/pod-product-compliance
Lightning Source LLC
Chambersburg PA
CBHW051358110526

44592CB00023B/2876